SOMETHING GOOD ON THE TABLE

Practical Proverbs for the Soul

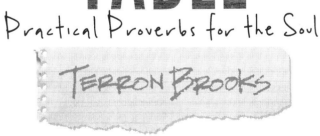

TERRON BROOKS

DEDICATION

This book is dedicated to my parents,
Wendell and Alicia Brooks.

My first true inspirations.

.

Acknowledgments

This book would not be possible without the gentle leading of God who prompted me to write it in the first place. So glad I listened.

Special thanks to **Chariya Bissonette**, whose encouragement pushed this book to completion. To **Thomas Clark**, for being my dream collaborator and visionary adding so much beauty to my thoughts. To **Rev Run**, for the outstanding example of pushing others to greatness. Last, but never least, my entire family for unconditional love that gives me the wide open space to fly to heights I never imagined possible.

To **Leilani**, my life's running mate. There aren't words beautiful, poetic, or accurate enough to describe my gratitude for your patience, endurance, and strength all of these amazing years together. Thank you, Wonder Woman, for everything.

To my own personal cheerleading squad who has picked me up from every fall or set back and has stood with me for every victory-**Michael and Christine Swanson**, **Sylvia MacCalla**, **Kamilah Marshall**, **Jerry Motto**, **Reegan Haynes**, and **Trudie Abraham**

TABLE OF CONTENTS

ENOUGH

Now is the time, pick up the pieces of your life
The tears you cried are rivers that have all run dry
You've gone to long, making misery company
The cuts you have, no longer do you see them bleed

Somebody should have told you, nobody can control you
That you have got the power to step out of the grave
You're gonna make it happen when faith becomes an action
When fear becomes subtracted from your heart
You're gonna say

Enough
Life is too short to spend another day
Caught up
Wishing your life had gone another way

Somebody wants to love you
Somebody wants to care
Somebody wants to tell you, Everything will be okay
You're gonna make it happen
You're gonna make it there
When you decide that enough is enough

Taken from my record #LoveMusic

GRATITUDE

PARK CITY, UTAH (DISNEY IN CONCERT) 1/16/14

The second you opened your eyes this morning,
you had the privilege of experiencing a miracle.
How will you choose to spend the amazing
beginning of an incredible moment?
Don't ever discount the first second of the day.
It's the origin of a jump start to something great.
Anything can happen today.
You ready?

Don't interrupt the gorgeous day you've
been given with an ugly attitude.

When faith becomes an action and
fear becomes subtracted from your
heart you'll be able to live with your
own life without getting caught up,
always wishing it was someone else's.

Miracles overwhelm the owner
of a thankful heart.

BELIEVE

I'm gonna put my FAITH back in my mouth
Gonna tell my feet the time is now
I'm gonna shatter all the glass upon the ceiling
I'm gonna give my soul a fighting chance
I know it hurts, I'm still gonna dance
I know the truth and it goes deeper than my feelings

And I've settled this in my heart

I will Believe, more than I can dream
Reach the forest through the trees and seize what's
meant for me
I will Believe, beyond what I can see
To unlock the door to life, you need the key
Believe

Taken from my record #LoveMusic

FAITH

NASHVILLE, TN (SHOOTING THE FILM HAV FAITH) 4/3/16

Faith stretches the road out in front of you
and leads you to horizons your eyes
would never see without it.

Turn off all of the voices that say it is not possible
and tune into God's voice that says it is.

Don't waste your energy on worry.
Use your energy to believe.

Prayers aren't just empty words.
God hears them and transforms
them into miracles.

Trust God even when
you can't trace Him.

FAITH

Although you may be waiting for God to respond,
there is no delay in hearing you when you call.
Trust the split second you reach out, He has
undoubtedly received your message.

Since God is an expert at Anything,
you can trust Him with Everything.

Trusting God doesn't mean
keeping your options open.

Surrendering to Christ does not mean
the end of everything you've dreamed of.
It's the beginning of greater things
you've never imagined.

You should look like you had work done
because God gives the best faith lifts.

Unbelieving prayers are
wasted moments with God.

Life is sweeter with the seasoning of faith.
Bitterness creeps in with the reasoning
of how God makes His decisions.
He's the Master Chef.
Everything He makes is good!

God's going to take care of
every little bit of it.

There is more than one basket
to hold your eggs.

You know what happens when we do nothing.
Nothing. Faith works.

IF WE LOVED

Nothing unites the heart like LOVE, nothing unites
the heart
Nothing divides a heart in love
Love's the place to start

Nothing ignites the heart like love, nothing ignites the heart
Nothing excites a heart like love
Let love make it's mark

If I loved you, wanting nothing in return
And if you loved me, beyond what I deserve
What that make a difference, tell me would it save us
If we loved?

If you loved me without a second thought
And if I loved you without counting up the cost
What a beautiful image, what a perfect finish
If we loved.

Taken from my record #LoveMusic

21

LOVE

CENTURY CITY, CA (14TH WEDDING ANNIVERSARY, DATE NIGHT WITH MY WIFE, LEILANI) 5/11/17

God wants to breathe His thoughts into your being.
He wants to show you His heart.
His love wants to speak for itself today.

LOVE

God's love is the ultimate
stain remover.

Plant yourself in God's love
and watch how much you grow.

If love was based on logic,
we would think our way out of it.

Love God first and then out of that
love will come your action.

God's love for you doesn't exist
whether you feel it or not. It's just there.
Your feelings cannot control
how He feels about you.
As you accept the air you
breathe today, accept God's love.
It's just as certain as the sun.

To be on God's side, you must be
on the Love side of things.

Check your love levels. Fill up daily so you
can cover someone else who is low.

When you stop running in circles,
God will be waiting in the center of it all.

When you find people who are
starving for love, feed them.

Whether you feel it or not,
God's love is never absent.
Because He IS love, when you access Him,
you instantly know the greatest love possible.
Let His love magnify what is
right with your life today.

God never gets tired of loving you.

You don't have to be perfect to receive
the perfect love of Christ.

Do you ever think that the thing
that is blocking you may be the very thing
protecting you from something you
don't even know you don't need.

When facing offense, Forgiveness is your defense.

The ego wants to know and control everything.
Love, just wants to give.

Nothing intimidates God.
So all of our excuses for not
bringing our lives to Him are void.
There's not a reason we can think of
that could ever challenge His love because
His grace covers Everything.

Who do you need to forgive today?
You might be on the top of your list.

God's love wants to furnish your heart.
Will you let Him decorate your life?

God's love is generous.
Help yourself!

If you see or hear somebody needing rescue,
don't ignore them, especially if
you have the answer.

Your hand is God's hand for
someone who needs a hand.

Praying for others is the best way
to bless yourself.

There's nothing greater than having God as
your inheritance. His love never runs out.

Life can sometimes be a blink.
May you continue to love every second
your eyes are open.

Before you become indignant with
the hate and intolerance in your neighbor,
eradicate all of it from yourself.
See how much time you have left.

Judging others for what they do, should do,
or not do, is counterproductive to love.
Love is needed where people are, not
where we think they should be.
That's the kind of love we'd want in return.
Let your love cover not strangle.

If Love is a light and you see darkness in
the world around you, why wouldn't you shine?
When you've tried everything else,
turn yourself ON.

MORE OF YOU

More of you in me
More of you in me
Want the world to see
More of you than me

More of you
Let them see your reflection
More of you
Help me love like you would
More of you
Want to make a connection with the
power that lives within

Taken from my record Contagious

WISDOM

NEW YORK, NY (THE SURVIVOR TREE/NATIONAL
SEPTEMBER 11 MEMORIAL) 1/16/15

Do you want to stand out?
Then step down. Be a servant.
Make your life count.

Keeping our expectations in God moves us
away from unrealistic expectations of others.

Aim to do what is right not
just what's convenient.

Don't be an obstacle for God's blessing
in your own life or the lives of others.

In all of your striving to get,
remember every perfect gift comes from above.
If it's yours, you'll get it. Breathe.

Be prepared. Opportunity knocks
when you least expect it.

God's word is an indispensable weapon.
Use it for the battle called life
and there is no way you can lose.

Open up your life. The smallness you feel
comes from within. Your life is not small
but you are living it in small ways.

Make today count for something
and tomorrow will be thankful you did.

Try not to over think everything,
it squeezes the joy out of life.
Leave room for surprises.
Tomorrow will take care of itself.

When you keep your eyes on God,
whom no eye can see, your eyes are actually
opened and you see far greater than before.

Set your clock to God's timing.

Don't leave talking with God out of
your daily routine. A little taste of heaven
will keep you on the right track.

Don't just let God rule.
Let him overrule you too.

Sometimes it's just not about what you get,
just give because you've been
blessed to have something.

Our actions are permanent but how
we feel about them don't have to be.
Forgive and move forward with
the lesson as a badge not a stain.

If it's not the truth,
don't entertain it.

Sometimes our badges of accolades are
barriers in the way of people seeing the real us.
Don't store up things that distract you from shining
bright like God, who reveals who you really are.

The most successful are
the most disciplined.

Don't let being right get you into
the wrong kind of trouble. It's a trap to place
your justice above integrity and Grace.

The surest way to get yourself into trouble
is to make pleasing others your god.
Even the good intention of making people happy can
rob us of our purposes in life
when we forfeit our Truth, Vision, and Integrity.
To thine own self be true and prayerfully
those around you will find a pathway
to happiness by example.

Put less energy into being relevant
and more into being real.

The smartest ones know it's smart
not to say everything that comes
to their smart minds.

Don't let the length of your journey
stifle the life out of your joy.

When we get overwhelmed, we tend
to overthink and create outrageous scenarios
that steal our breath in the moment.
God has already looked at your situation
and has charted a course for you.
Keep Him close and you
won't miss the boat.

You don't lose anything
by cheering someone else on.

Bringing out the best in others
brings out the best in yourself.

When we want to put people in their place,
it's good to remember it's their place.
Whether we like it or not,
it's their choice to make.
Don't let their position get
you out of your place.

Take a look at your motives today.
Why are you doing what you are doing?
Results are based on your intentions.

There is a huge difference between
being a servant and being a slave.
There is no shame in setting boundaries.

There's always great rewards when
taking the high road.

The path to glory is on
the wings of humility.

Want to avoid regret?
Keep your heart in step with God's directions.
It's so easy to veer off the course
that God has set for us.
To hold steady would mean to give up our
own plans and keep our eyes on our own roads,
roads paved by Him, especially for us.
In the seconds it takes to try a short cut,
we can find ourselves spinning out of control.

Let your life be the pie and your
accomplishments the cherries.
Not, the other way around.

GREEN LIGHT (GO!)

You can't believe 'till and you see
what's right in front of you
You go through life like any moment you might fall
Walking around with no clue,
it's you you're running from
Looking for a sign to tell you what to do
What are you waiting for?

Green light Go
It's your time and you got to go
Ready, set, go
It's your life and you gotta go

Why are you waiting
The light is changing
Your destiny is right in front of you
Stop hesitating
Freedom is waiting
There's nothing in your way
Just make your move

Taken from my record Contagious

FEAR
IDYLWILD, CA (BROOKS FAMILY VACATION) 1/2/18

Resist making fear your choice today.
God wants to give you peace beyond
understanding but He won't force it on you.
Peace IS possible but it begins with belief.
Maybe you just need to decide, change the
course of your thinking, and receive.
We all have to find a place to put our fear.
God's hands are big enough for all of them.

Deflect fiery fear with fearless faith.

The "worst" is never the worst.
God specializes in the impossible.

Don't be afraid to sing your own song.
Let your soul give you your round of applause.
It's not to be judged.

Your spirit is counting on you to cultivate
the neighborhood it resides around.
It'll cost you more to stay where you
are not challenged than to move to a
place where love expects more
of you and raises you up.
Sometimes safe is another
word for stuck.

When Jesus represents you,
you can command fear to be gone.
Your rolodex is useless without that name.

The very heavens were handcrafted by God
and you think He won't take care of you?

God promises to go with us.
Our problem is we don't GO.

Since there is not a day in your future
that God won't be there,
you can truly live right now with no fear.

Faith is the only permanent mark
that puts a line through fear.

TRUTH
SANTA BARBARA, CA 11/17/16

God isn't keeping you alive by accident.
There's a reason why you're still here.

Nobody is capable of self help.
We lie too much to ourselves.
But God knows the root of
where our need begins.
Put Him on retainer and
see how His Word sticks.

Probably is not in God's vocabulary.

We cannot out plan God.
Prayer and praise are more
important than planning.

Anxiety can be infectious.
Nervous energy spreads like a wild fire.
Avoid being a cloud of smoke
in someone's blue sky.
Think positively before
you speak prematurely.

Being addicted to other people's business
leaves your own unfinished.

Lights don't shine unless they are turned on.
Be intentional about how you respond
to the darkness in this world.
We become what we worship.

The people you look up to should
not obstruct your view from God.
There is no vacancy at the top spot.
The position has been filled and the
Highest seat is occupied, permanently.

Life will never be perfect but
God's ways forever will be.
We just have to follow directions.

Bringing out the best in others
brings out the best in yourself.

God cannot be our hope AND
our source of frustration.
Until you resolve what you believe,
you'll never be satisfied.
The only way to get off the
seesaw of life is to stop
complaining and just trust.

You won't lose time
if you use it wisely.

You can be alive and
dead at the same time.
But when God invades your life,
death takes a back seat.
You may have tried everything
but God is a sure thing.
Everything that is dead in your
life will awaken in His light.

Life can be messy. God is
not intimidated by mess.
We only need to be humble
enough to recognize we can't
clean it all up on our own.
God specializes in putting
chaos back into order.
Let him help you recover your
joy from all the clutter.

You're never sorry when you
knock on God's door.

God takes no pleasure in making life hard,
in throwing roadblocks in your
way for you to stumble.
It's easy to blame God for everything.
The more angry we are at God,
the further apart from Him we grow.
Let the pressures of life
cause you to run into Him.
There's always a clear
path into His arms.

God says not only do
you belong to Him.
He belongs to you.

"You can't please everybody."
Didn't mama say this more
than a hand full of times.
Time to listen.

Do yourself a favor and give
God a listening ear today.
Sometimes we can talk
ourselves out of the truth.
God won't lie to you.

When God desires to create more
power in your life, you may
experience more friction.

You might not fit in and that's ok.

Negativity is the harvest of
insecurities running wild.
Trust the Giver, not the gift.
It's ok that you're not perfect,
nobody is.

Your mistake is a perfect beginning
for your Miracle.

Chase discipline like you
chase your dreams.
The bigger the dream,
the stronger you need to be.

When God restores He ALWAYS
returns what is lost in better
condition than you had it.
(Actually He makes all things NEW).
So dry up those tears
over your spilled milk.

Might not be worth doing if it
causes you to grumble.

Judging others throws the swiftest
boomerang in your own back.

You won't be able to use the old attitude
for the new things God is doing.
He's Big so think Big!

What you want will present itself when
the true you shows up to get it.
What's for you is for you and not
who you're pretending to be.

You are not what happened to
you but what happened to you
has made you who you are.

Every battle's victory depend on
the root of our trust in God.

Since God has qualified you,
don't let anybody count you out!

TRUTH

Haters can hurt us or humble us.
Try not to be surprised when people don't think
you are as wonderful as you think you are.
It doesn't mean you're not. Its just not unanimous.

The only way you sink is by
letting go of God's hand.
Sailing may not be smooth all of the
time but His palm is the safest
boat out on the harbor.

The true desires of our hearts come to
the surface when we get excited
about God's sovereignty.

Distractions overcome the disconnected.
Lose focus, lose your way. Eyes on God.
Eyes on Glory.

How often do we put God
in the tiniest box while
expecting the biggest blessings.

Free yourself of self consciousness.
People are going to think what
they think of you anyway.
God's thoughts trumps them all and He
absolutely loves you the way you are.

Without peace,
there is no success.

God's Presence deserves more
Praise than his Performance.

If you allow God to reign over your life,
you'll never have to worry about
missing His blessing.

Gentleness takes practice.

Creating boundaries for yourself
only creates division with people
who do not love you.

Reality check.
Sometimes you can't do it all.
And it's okay.

Knowing you matter to the One that
matters most is what matters.

TRUST
BALDWIN HILLS, CA (COPPER HOUSE)

The very first step in relying on God is:
DO nothing.

A catastrophe happens between the time
the very bad thing happened and the time
you decide to handle it without God.

You don't have to lie to God.
The truth won't hurt Him.
What grieves Him most is our inability to
accept that He already knows all truth anyway.
So run through the fields of His love
while trampling shame under your feet.
You don't have to pretend to have it all together.
God's got it from here.

The very heavens were handcrafted by God
and you think He won't take care of you?

If we continue fighting battles which are God's,
of course we keep getting hurt.
Put your sword down today and be at peace
with your Champion who wins every fight.

Getting ahead of yourself is getting ahead of God.
While you're ahead there is a vacant spot
in the present where you have not
allowed God to do His planned work.
Stay in the moment today.

Don't hold anything back from God
and watch what he puts in your hands.

Believe me. God takes you seriously.
Your life and concerns are not up in the air.
Everything falls into his hand.

You can make it through anything
in the One who made you who you are.
God who makes everything work together will
work you into his most excellent harmonies.

God does His best stitching when
everything comes apart at the seams.

Don't be afraid to take a break.
You can't be everywhere.
You can't say yes to everything.
You can't make every dollar.
You can't fight every cause.
You can't save everybody.
You can't run from yourself or you will Break.
You'll only be missing out on all of these things
if you aren't 100% present to enjoy them.
Respect yourself.
Take more than a day off.
God's amazing blessing
and grace never run out.
You have His permission.
Rest.

You can celebrate the rescue of God
because certainly it's on the way.

Let God handle your affairs the first time.
Don't ask him to undo what
you started without him.

You can't just give God an hour of your trust.
The other 23 hours will worry you to death.

God knows where you are and
knows where you are going.

You don't need to know what God is going to do.
Just that He's going to do something.
He does all things well.

God will complete in detail
what He's decided about you.
And all His decisions are good.

GRACE
CLEVELAND, OH (I CAN'T MAKE YOU LOVE ME, STAGE PLAY) 12/17/17

God's grace opens like a flower.
One day(petal) at a time.

God's Grace wants to be the
roof over your head today.
Walk confidently in the safety of His love.

God hasn't lost track of you.
He's got a Light on you that doesn't burn out.
No matter how fast or far you run,
without catching His breath,
He's already there.
Even on days when you lag behind,
His patience doesn't know
how to run thin.

Don't be surprised when God blesses
you despite what you've done.
His grace extends beyond perfect performances.

Being good doesn't put you ahead of others.
Our need for God keeps us in the same place.
Goodness never cancels grace.

Don't make a habit of finding fault in others.
If you're looking for something to do,
try finding a little grace when
dealing with difficult people.

The weeds in your life are not always
to blame for our stunted progression.
Sometimes we've let things go without noticing
we haven't left the same spot for some time.
Might be time to reevaluate our landscapes and
make some changes that benefit our gardens.
Grace never stalls growth.
It gives us permission to be trees.

The sweetest of life's lessons in grace
sometimes come from the most
rotten of life's experiences.

Forgive someone's debt today.
Wash it clean.
You've been waiting for a repayment long
enough with no evidence it will be repaid.
Get the anxious time back by letting it go.
The gift you gave will come back in wisdom.
Remove the tension and angst in what belongs
to you not getting back in your hands.
God saw it and has a better repayment plan.
Be free, now.

IDENTITY
SOHO, NEW YORK (MATTHEW
MORRISON CONCERT) 10/15/17

PRIDE
SANTA BARBARA, CA

Stop waiting for someone
to tell you who you are!

If you underestimate yourself,
how do you expect others to value who you are?
Discount yourself and others will too.
Don't sell yourself short and make
people see you at full price.

Sometimes we focus on what we are
not that we forget who we are.

Let the knowledge of who God says
you are trump every other person
and every other thing.

The world can never give
you true significance.
Find God.
Find yourself.

Let go that ego.
It's humility that exalts you.
You'll be lifted up as you live to serve others.
A proud heart cannot sustain happiness.
It's always looking for more.

PRIDE

It's hard enough living up
to the opinions of others.
The true trap is setting your
own of yourself too high.
It's impossible to have compassion
for someone else when we've
used it up on ourselves.

PRIDE

Don't always seek to be consoled
but make it your mission to console others
and in turn watch yourself get lifted up.

Don't confuse your greatness
with the Greatness of God inside of you
which gives you the power to be Great.

WON'T BACK DOWN

It was your mission to get me to see
I'd never end up where I want to be
But I have climbed a mountain, been tossed by the sea
Nothing you can do now
Will get the best of me

No, I won't back down
If it hasn't killed me
It's too late now
No, I won't lie down
What was meant to break me
Saved me somehow

It may be impossible, uncomfortable
I'm focused on my goal
Disappointments are inevitable, they break the soul
They're only meant for growth
But I can feel invincible
Because I know
I'm not going down
Not now, not now

Taken from my record Contagious

STRENGTH
BERMUDA ISLANDS 3/4/17

SURRENDER
BERMUDA ISLANDS 3/4/17

God's power is at the
end of your rope.

You don't win by human strength or intellect.
You win by overcoming through
the Source of all power,
which cannot be defeated.

Focus on your strengths and let God
deal with your weaknesses.

Trusting takes supernatural power.
Thank God His power is free
and available upon request.
Fuel up today.

Need some adrenaline for your soul?
God's word will sky
rocket you into orbit.

God's plan for you is not just survival but victory.
Be an overcomer today!

Ask God today to make you more.
You've been getting by but
now it's time to soar.
God assigns you the wings to rise
above the storms of life.

When we plug into Jesus,
we never lose power.

Inner strength only works when
what's inside of you is strong.
No good is a built body with a weak heart.
Don't ignore your inner man.
The mirror puts on a good show.

The power is yours today.
Let your attitude reflect your resilience.
You are a winner.
God gave you another day
to remind you of this.

If you want God to be hands on,
you've got to take your hands off.

You cannot receive
until you surrender.

God wants to bless you.
This is no secret.
How he does it is the mystery.
His ways may seem strange but
there is only one wise God.
Let him have his way with you
and through you, today.

It's when we get tired of figuring it out
THEN God begins to show us the way.

Let "Thy will be done" be more
of a song today than a sigh.

Making room for God in our lives is
insulting at the very least since He actually
built the house we call our bodies.
Stop changing the locks on
THE LandLord and let love in.

Let your tears be rivers that carry
you away into God's presence.

You were born to shine.
However, there is a designated place God has
set for you wherein your light shines brightest.
Will you glow where He tells you to go?

You will be free to forgive when
you release your will to God.

The outcomes are not up to you.
Leave them in the hands of God.

SURRENDER

When you stop trying to contain
God's goodness and grace in your life,
the rush of the overflow will not only
take you higher than you imagined but will
sweep those around you up as well.
The spill is inevitable.
Go with it!

GET BACK UP AGAIN

What do you say to a brand new
day full of new beginnings
Move out of your way, here's your
chance no looking back
What would you do if I told you
life was worth the living
To silence the lies and and embrace the fact

Get Back Up Again
You spread your wings and then you fly, high
Sky is your limit
It only happens when you use your
STRENGTH and then, you know
There is nothing stopping you
From getting back up again

Taken from my record Contagious(Deluxe)

PATIENCE
SANTA BARBARA, CA 11/17/16

PERSERVERANCE
PORTLAND, OR

Instead of hitting the panic button today,
push the patience button.
Things are going to work out.
Might not be the way you've planned but
what's the chance they may work out better?
Just wait a second.

The work God does within us while
we wait is just as important as
whatever it is we're waiting for.

We can learn to wait on God,
as many times as he has to wait on us.

No matter what's going on,
do yourself a favor and be
patient, pleasant, and kind.

Be slower to speak.
Be careful where you point your finger.
Be more concerned about
matters of the heart.
And be more of a reflection
than a blind spot.

Waiting isn't useless.
A spirit needs time to enlarge.
Every second counts.

Are you stuck trying to get to the next level?
Try getting on God's altitude.
When you get there, you will appreciate
the level you are on and you'll find peace
while you're waiting to ascend.

Prayers aren't over when we stop talking.
Take some time to listen today.

Waiting on God is easy because He
knows when the waiting ends.

The crown of a winner is sometimes
weaved from pain and suffering.

Much of the success in your life has
less to do with what God has allowed
you to achieve but with what God
has helped you to endure.

Make your problem be your platform.

You can only persevere with
the dependence on God.
You'll never make it by yourself.

COMFORT IN YOUR PLAN

Through the adversity, I can find rest in your peace
There's a calm over me, right where I am
And through the uncertainty,
I'm right where you want me to be
I've learned I can hear you speak
Right where I am

I know the plans you have for me
Plans you have for me to succeed
So I don't worry, I just take your hand
Find comfort in your plan

I know the thoughts you think of me
Thoughts you have to prosper me
So I don't worry, I can just stand
There's comfort in your plan

Taken from my record Contagious

PEACE
Boise, ID

HEALING
Hawaii, HI

Don't let negative thoughts
hold you hostage today.
In the split seconds you have to
give in to them, make them
surrender to the Light.
They must behave when
God walks in the room.

PEACE

Sometimes you have to silence all
of the voices to hear your own.

Unpack the baggage from yesterday so that you can receive the peace of God that is waiting to invade today.

Take a break worrying about your
future garden and smell the roses
that are right in front of you.

The wise men followed a star which
led them straight to Jesus.
Don't forget you are a walking star.
Who are you leading with your light today?
Your love should glow.
Anybody wise enough to look
for Peace shouldn't have to
look too far to find you.

The happiest people don't
have the most perfect lives.
What they have is perfect peace
with the lives they've been given.
Their joy is rooted deep within where the
outside world's inconsistencies can't choke it out.
The only condition is when the well within dries up.
Thank God He is the thirst quencher, a free
flowing ocean in the worst droughts.

The world can never give
you true significance.
Find God.
Find yourself.

What God prescribes has
no negative side effects.

God can use your brokenness to bring
wholeness to someone else.
That's what he did with
his son Jesus, for you.

Don't let what hurt you hinder
you from your harvest.

If you wanna be healed, forgive.

I'LL BE LOVING YOU

Even though the rain may fall
Even when the fire burns
You're feeling there's no hope at all
I'll be loving you

That's what I'll do
When you need a shoulder
That's what I'll do
When you need a friend
I will hold you
When you think you're life is over
Always remember
I'll be loving you

Even while your earth is shaking
Even as your spirit aches
Know that there is no mistaking
I'll be loving you

I can't help it
I won't change it
It's how I feel, because it's real
I'll stay
You can't earn it
You won't hurt it away
It's how I feel, because it's real
Never go away

Even though the doors are closing
Even when you've lost your way
Even where no words are spoken
I'll be loving you

Taken from my record Contagious

ENCOURAGEMENT

NASHVILLE, TN (SHOOTING THE FILM HAV FAITH) 4/4/16

God speaks so highly of you.
Everything he has said about you will
do the work he has sent them to do.
His Word concerning you will accomplish
the destiny he has put in place for you.
It's up to you to agree with
what He has said.

No, is the best yes for something else.

In time, your pain will prove
to you its purpose.

God doesn't need an eraser.
His plan for you is sure and settled.
He gets it right on the first draft.

Don't try and keep up with others.
During the race, just keep up with God.
He's waiting for you at the finish line.

While waiting for your ship to come in,
there is a boat at the dock with your name on it.
Sometimes big finishes take small starts.

God is never overwhelmed.

Nothing surprises God.
He's not caught off guard.
He looks straight through your situation
and always sees Victory.

God sometimes delays the fulfillment
of the promise but never
the promise itself.

Don't be so hard on yourself.
Your humanness magnifies God's godliness.

Your dream started with God's dream for you.
When He sets your course, the reality
of your dream is as sure as
the stars you wish upon.

An encouraging word can save someone's life.
Don't hesitate to give one Today!

God turns life around.

God can go before you and be
with you at the same time.

Taking responsibility for our own actions teaches
others to take a look at their own.

A compliment can be a whisper from God.
Don't make people pay for them.
Give them away for free.

MOMENT IN YOUR LIFE

Life is hard
There is pain
Can't escape
These moments in your life
But one day, things will change
Scars will fade
It's just a moment in your life

Be open, keep HOPING
You will get through the night
Be open, keep holding on
Everything will be alright

Taken from my record Contagious

HOPE
HAWAII, HI

Hope expects.

God specializes in nick
of time deliveries.

It's hard to have high hopes when we bring
God down to the level of our understanding.
So trust today beyond the barriers of your
mind to see just how far faith can soar.

Negative talk eventually traps
you in a web of impossibility.
Release yourself by speaking Hope filled words.
God can only endorse and enforce The Truth.

Lights don't shine unless they are turned on.
Be intentional about how you respond
to the darkness in this world.

Regardless, God has not
misplaced his glory.

Your Now was set, Then.

CONTAGIOUS

Now that I've caught this JOY
I don't mind spreading my disease
I want you to know the effect it has on me
If you free your heart you'll find it's always there
You can't run away, love's in the air

And it's contagious, the way that I feel
It's outrageous, to know that it's real
It's so amazing, can't keep it to myself
Cause it's contagious
I wanna give it to somebody else

Can you feel it?

Life is but a frame unless
Jesus is in the picture.

Taken from my record Contagious

JOY
PASADENA, CA (VIDEO SHOOT FOR
MY SONG CONTAGIOUS) 2014

JOY

Don't give fun a back seat.
There will always be burdens to
consume you and stir you crazy.
It's up to you what you let drive.
Let joy be the fuel to get you through.

Stop waiting for the other shoe
to drop and just Be Happy!

Life is but a frame unless
Jesus is in the picture.